Grace Notes

Grace Notes

Poems about Families

NAOMI SHIHAB NYE

Greenwillow Books

An Imprint of HarperCollinsPublishers

Grace Notes: Poems about Families

Copyright © 2024 by Naomi Shihab Nye

harpercollinschildrens.com

The text of this book is set in 10-point Iowan Old Style.
Book design by Paul Zakris
Interior illustrations by Lynne Avril

Library of Congress Cataloging-in-Publication Data

Names: Nye, Naomi Shihab, author.
Title: Grace notes : poems about families / Naomi Shihab Nye.
Description: First edition. | New York : Greenwillow Books, 2024. |
Includes index. | Audience: Ages 13 up. | Audience: Grades 7-9. |
Summary: A collection of poems about family and the love we share with one another throughout life's peaks and valleys.
Identifiers: LCCN 2024004872 (print) | LCCN 2024004873 (ebook) |
ISBN 9780062691873 (hardcover) | ISBN 9780062691897 (ebook)
Subjects: LCSH: Children's poetry, American. | Family life—Poetry. |
CYAC: American poetry. | Family life—Poetry. | LCGFT: Poetry.
Classification: LCC PS3564.Y44 G73 2024 (print) | LCC PS3564.Y44 (ebook) |
DDC 811/.54—dc23/eng/20240228
LC record available at https://lccn.loc.gov/2024004872
LC ebook record available at https://lccn.loc.gov/2024004873
24 25 26 27 28 LBC 5 4 3 2 1
First Edition

Greenwillow Books

In honor of Miriam Naomi Allwardt Shihab (1927–2021)

Table of Contents

PART TWO:
Sometimes We Need a Bigger Family

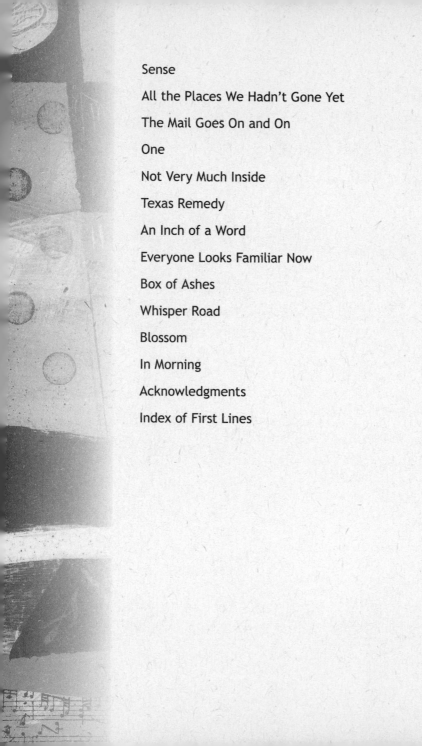

The small things I love, have they any weight?
So many dialects of green.
And especially the red of housewalls.
—Tomas Tranströmer, from "The Open Window"

It is very strange . . . that I had a mother. Sometimes
I think that I dreamed her too much. I dreamed her so much
that I made her. Almost all mothers are creatures of our dreams.
—Jaime Sabines, from "Doña Luz"

A Zen monk wearing a black robe and carrying a clipboard,
asked me if I was Edie.
I thought he said "eating."
Not now, I said.

Introduction

Families. They're our first circle. We wake up to them as babies, clicking into focus, identifying, absorbing . . . forever discovering who they are.

Who we think they are is only one little window.

It's always a shock to realize your parent had a full life before you were even born.

Tribe, community, ground zero, baseline, starting point. Easy and hard and mysterious, all at once. You can think you know everything there is to know about a person, but this is never true.

Writing about families is one of the richest topics we have, though I was twenty before I realized this. Until then, I had written about everything else: cats, friends, moods, neighborhoods, loss, weather. The topic arrived for me one day in my university library when I started writing notes about a grumpy older cousin, who was disapproving of me at that moment. I remember feeling so cheered by making those notes, it suddenly seemed my body of writing material had vastly expanded.

Later, when working with kids, I used to begin some writing

workshops with a two-thousand-year-old poem by a poet named Vishnavath, from India. We guessed Vishnavath was a young boy, but weren't sure. Each of Vishnavath's family members was described through a single metaphor. The mother was a river tending all her tiny streams. The brother was a packhorse carrying burdens. The sister, a doll in a soiled dress. Vishnavath ended with "And I, a kettle of water boiling away into steam."

I would invite the kids to write about their own families (they could include grandparents, aunts, uncles, cousins, etc.) in a similar fashion—stacking the lines—and ending with themselves.

Also, if they preferred, they could focus on only one family member and list various metaphors for that person. An "easy assignment" was how I thought of this, and the students always seemed to enjoy it, wanting to share their poems afterward, often asking if they could write another one at home. Sometimes the poems veered off into "difficult material"—one father was a liquor store, but his vodka bottles were thrown all over the floor, not lined on a shelf. I worried about this one, when the student wanted to read it at a reading, even discussing it with the principal, who said, "This young writer is telling his truth!"

And I kept trying to do it myself. After my father died sixteen years ago, I worked on poems for a book about him called *Transfer*

(BOA Editions Ltd., 2011), and found the project comforting and enlightening. I even used some of my dad's own floating sentences from his notebooks as titles in one section. My mom said, "Hey, what about me?"

After she died in 2021, I worked on *Grace Notes*. It seemed we were continuing our long, long conversation, as the writer/translator Alastair Reid once described the ongoing dialogue after someone dies. Of course, I had already been taking notes about my mother all my life. Working on some of these poems really made me laugh.

Sometimes, writing about something makes it seem funny for the first time.

All my life, I collected quotes like "The ground beneath your feet is not stable" (Grand Teton National Park) and "It is strange to be here. The mystery never leaves you alone" (John O'Donohue, Ireland). They really helped me feel better when times were rough. It's easy to take notes. My suggestion would be to take them always, not just in class.

My friend Linda, a ceramic artist, fires pots in her mother's own old kiln. Blue-gray glazes emerge, with a haunting depth. Maybe we are all born from our mothers' kilns. Certain shapes of being, thoughts, and ideas, will stay with us no matter what we do.

Unexpectedly, voices will pop into our dreams and our days. Why not use them? Let them speak again?

I honor my beautiful, brave mother and know she might take issue with a few of my perspectives, but that's okay. We were always very open and free in our conversations. I hope that anyone who reads these poems has occasion to think about their own family members even more than mine. It's our lifetime project. It helps us keep living.

Naomi Shihab Nye
San Antonio, Texas, 2024

PART ONE

No Age Is Empty

How Parents Ever Get Together Anyway

They might grow up on opposite sides of the world.
Different religions, different foods . . .
then one day they come to a town in Kansas,
take jobs in the same psychiatric hospital,
neither of them doctors . . .
yes, sure, that sounds likely!
The only thing they had in common was
hope
and open minds.

He wore a white jacket
down to his knees.
In the wedding picture
she looks taller than he is,
actually they were the same size.
Born the same year. Two sides of the earth.
Sure! Let's get married in three months, why not?

What about you? How did your parents
end up in the same spot?
Was it obvious?
Did they live on the same block?
Did they like each other from the first minute?
Did they turn away in first grade?

My father-to-be told a bystander,
I'm going to marry that girl.
The man said, Then you're crazier than I am.

A seedpod flies through the air.
Nighthawks lay their eggs in gravel.
A butterfly migrates across borders with no papers.
A turtle returns to the same beach.

The fact we exist at all
is a random grace note
of a forgotten symphony.

Mother Muscle

So many questions you will want to ask your mother.

Where all her dresses went.

How she knew so much, about every single subject.

She read Emily Dickinson to me when I was three.
The poems were short. She could read one,
then read it again if I asked.

But what made her take that book off the library shelf
to begin with?

She was a painter, not a poet.
Still, she knew words better
than I ever would.

No "me and him,"
no "ain't,"
in her presence.
Once she wrote to a TV program
called *Leave It to Beaver*
because Beaver said "ain't."
They wrote back, apologized.

‬

I worried my whole life she would die.

Did she worry I would die?

My friend Laila says motherhood love is a muscle
that gets strengthened in all times, beautiful and challenging.

I was born nine months and nine days
after my mother's wedding.
Was she ready?

Mother muscles become tough. They have to.
People pulling on them
all the time. Ferocious mamas
stomping through the tangled wilderness
searching for berries. Mamas worrying
night and day.

We want, we want, we want.
⚬
Who is your mother?
Some days, that tree is my mother.
When I paint, I become my mother.

Her hand inside my hand.
Her eyes inside mine.
But we see different things.

We traveled together from a far galaxy
and split into different generations when we got close
to Earth. Once, we were the same age.

We will be again.

Mother Anthem

Yes, no.
Maybe, maybe someday, maybe never,
you shouldn't, we might—
I still need to be taken care of, too.

A rocking cradle of notes
holds the restless child,
calms the flurry.
Now rest beneath night's shadow . . .
made shadow more a friend.
Unending, this song.
You will always need it.

My friends whose mothers died too young
lived very different lives.
We all live different lives, but this
deepest shadow
settling on the roof at night
was with them always,
only rising
when the world wrapped around them
in a warm enough way.

I saved my wedding dress,

stitched it myself,

heavy silk,

what will you ever do with it?

Living in a plastic bag.

No one wants to be hemmed in.

Map Factory

Somewhere a map of your life
is being drawn by a quiet hand in a noisy room.
A child steps off a bus in gray drizzle.
Elevator mouth opens,
the child presses 3 and rides up alone.
The child *is* three so she can remember this.
Mama stands at a tall gray table
in a room full of men.
She is sketching something on a large pad.
When she lifts the child up to show her,
the child sees crossing lines, dotted lines,
softly drawn.
Someday this map will be able to show a pilot
where to fly, Mama says excitedly.
Can you imagine it? What would
everything *look* like from a plane?
The child shakes her head.
The mother shakes her head.
She can't imagine it either.

Legacy

My whole life
would not have happened without
a man whose name I do not know
who died in the snow.
He was young,
had been married only three months
to my mama's best friend.

Walking on a wintry path in Kansas,
he toppled into a snowbank, dead.
That's it. All the information.

When he died so suddenly
my mama moved to the town
where his young bride lived,
to console her for a few months
as she got over the shock.

Her friend had a job,

so my future mama got a temporary job

selling sewing machines

and a volunteer job in a hospital,

where she met my dad

who had just landed

from the other side of the world.

See?

The snowbank.

The poor frozen man.

I owe him everything.

It Was Lace on a Life to Have a Mother

Think of it.
The idea of being.
Where it begins, then shifts.

Her voice inside you,
humming with stomach
and heart.

Crooning, singing,
reminding,
welling up like wind.

Slight cinnamon scent, texture
of skirt or trousers, when you
first start gripping on.

Watching her
to see
if she laughed.

The sweater
she is always
knitting.

For ten years!
With green mountains in it.
She is taking care of you.

You will be this way.
Someday you will have
patience.

She didn't mind mess,
my mother,
no, she gloried in it.

You
cleaned
it up.

Sides of the Family

Grandmothers, stretching back.
When do they click into focus?
Think how many you really had.
Picture them lined to the horizon.

One of my grandmothers prayed
five times a day. Talked to donkeys and cats
as if they were people. Laughed wildly,
urging everyone to bring her soft new
sweaters. Was a widow fifty years. Gave advice
if you asked or even didn't. When night felt too long,
lay still on her back and prayed.
For the cold darkness and the hopeful days.
Never bitter, despite being a refugee.
How would you like to lose your house?
Climbed a wooden ladder to the roof.
Believed in the sunset. Ate yogurt and cucumbers,
feared socks. Said socks make us weak.
Wore a white hijab, lived to 106,
always seemed young.

The other one on this side of the planet

tugged on nylon stockings, laced black shoes.

Kept hands tightly folded in her lap.

Never missed church. Bought me secret desserts.

And a giant doll who opened and closed

her eyes. I had asked for the doll.

This grandma had fluffy white hair,

grumpy husband, dark apartment.

Rode buses, stared into department store windows.

Didn't mention Bavaria, where her ancestors came from.

Always seemed old, often said, Never mind.

These grandmas did not meet. But I think there were little lines

between them like dotted ripples in a star constellation diagram.

Big Dipper, small dipper, they both shone down on us

all our lives. They were constants.

Now They Are Gone

The night before I was born
my mother and father
sleeping side by side
had the same dream,
that I came talking.
Fresh in a white cradle,
wrapped in soft baby cotton,
full sentences spilling from baby lips
onto the sheets.

Neither could remember what I said.

We would go on to talk
and talk for years,
calling each other daily,
writing a million letters,
Post-its, faxes, emails.
They each had
perfect grammar.

I Stood in My Crib

First memory:

clinging to the rail.

They were not happy in the living room.

Mama, Dada.

Two big people, hard words

bouncing back and forth.

Bodies rushing across the room,

arms waving.

They thought

I was sleeping.

I was wide awake.

Peering around the corner and afraid.

My little cloth diaper heavy,

no one paying attention to me.

I didn't know many words yet, but heard

their edges.

Union Boulevard, St. Louis

My mother's family came from Ohio,
then Illinois, her parents crossing a shining
Mississippi River
to settle in a city that had the blues,
always had the blues,
was born of the blues,
and they had the blues, too.

Blues were a baggage.
You could feel them when someone
walked into a room.

They carried their Germany with them,
heavier language, blue-and-white plates
but mostly the God-fearing behavior
she found so hard to take.
Sinner since birth? How so?
She stuffed those accusations
under her bed, with paints and brushes,
shoeboxes and dust.
She tied them in twine.
She said, *Not mine.*

They carried their Switzerland,
twenty below zero,
a general chill.
Something was missing.
Why would a person leave villages
of crystalline snow
to move to Ohio?

They did not
seem interested
in that person.
She was interested.

Something was always missing,
a crack in the story,
luggage with its contents leaked.

As a little girl at her grandmother's funeral,
my mother was threatened by her grandpa.
Do not cry, he said, poking a large finger in her face.
If I see you cry,
I will be very angry for a long time.

She didn't cry then,

but cried for the next sixty years,

and from what I understand,

he was usually angry anyway.

Her own grumpy father,

son of the angry preacher,

dragged his laundry in a wire cart

down the block at three a.m.

so he didn't have to see

other people.

I was mostly impressed that laundromats

stayed open all night,

but now I wonder . . .

who dislikes other people that much?

Who does chores in the dark?

Life

is full of mysteries.

They're not mine, not yours.

They're life's.

My Mom, Miriam Naomi

Her first name meant *bitter*.
How could anyone enjoy a name like that?
It's biblical, her parents said.
But she never liked it.

Later she passed on her middle name to me.
Naomi, also biblical, means *pleasant*,
used against me when I was a grouch.
Good luck it was also my father's
dead sister's name
so it belonged to both of them.
But did it belong to me?

At twelve I discovered
NAOMI backward was I MOAN.
This helped everybody.

Heavy Heads

At age twenty-one, Skowhegan Art School in Maine,

my mother chisels a self-portrait

in gray granite stone.

The gorgeous head weighs

two hundred fifty pounds.

She's not quite happy with it,

so starts a second one.

The heads will sit proudly in more than one yard.

She will not be able to take them

to Jerusalem, but the heads

will wait for us, so that thousands of miles later

and what feels like

thousands of years, the heads are sitting

in Texas under a bush

and near the bamboo. Are they friends?

The second pink granite head, which she always

described as unfinished,

was it the alter ego she never cared for?

The pink head has its chin on its arm.

The gray head will stare you down.
I think of my very thin mother
on a cross-country bus
lugging two heads that both look
like herself and how she explained this.

Pots and Pans

They lived together,

nestled inside one another,

never complained.

I loved their secret silver cabinet

in the bottom of the stove,

rings on their handles,

shiny faces.

The fitting

of the lids.

I pulled them in and out

for regular checks,

gave them names,

liked the little ones best.

Posing for Pictures at Two

Puffy pink dress
frilled at bottom
like a ballet tutu
made me cross my legs
raise arms
to the sides
little bird in flight
while cameras clicked
but then
I lost balance
toppled over
hit the fence.
Flowery pink vines
knotted in wires
my forehead hit a post
and swelled.
Never again
would I try to look fancy
in a picture because I knew
it could turn around
and hurt you.

Little Red Diary

Her impeccable handwriting documented

nearly every day, ages thirteen to seventeen.

Grandma said I could keep the book I'd found in a drawer,

so I didn't tell my mother for a while.

By then I had absorbed every page.

Church, movies, popcorn.

Bucky was important, whoever he was.

She washed her hair. Underlined <u>*No freedom at all.*</u>

I combed through soft yellow pages hungry for drama.

She got a new skirt! Her throat was sore!

One day Carroll almost fell out of his seat.

But who was Carroll?

Later (*News flash*) he came over for dinner and

dried the dishes. Movies cost ten cents.

She started college at sixteen and lived at home.

And she used the word "boring" which would be banned

from our own house. She even said, "very boring"

many days in a row. One summer afternoon

she found me soaking up her notes,

and grabbed the little red book back.

Mom, you said "boring"! Why can't we?

I gave you a better life, she said.

Better Life

We would know things, pronunciations of painters' names,
histories of composers,
how to steam vegetables instead of boiling them.
The word "organic" at a young age.
We would attend Bible School to know the stories,
not to be more holy than others.

My mother was a seeker all her life.
She cared about people far away,
the ones we couldn't see. She wanted them
to have enough to eat.

She never thought she was
the center of the world.

Were we able to imagine
the Volga, the Danube, the Nile,
artists dipping paintbrushes,
sculptors chipping away with small chisels,
farmers in yellow fields,
hay wagons,
goat herds,
avalanches,
what people survived?
The sorrow of Van Gogh?

Could we picture fruit on a wooden table
in France?

No one was stuck
if you entered an image,
felt suspended by color,
blue merging to green,
light on a clay pottery dish.
yellow-toned,
almost like butter.

Shelbyville, Illinois

Every summer my mother's parents left their grim city apartment
to return to the old house in the small town.

Grandma stirred succotash in enamel pans.
Grandpa snored on the back porch stacked with newspapers.

I was entranced by the tall clean rooms, polished wood,
tight upholstery, unused closets where ghosts lived.

My mama meditated in the garden, eyes closed, hands open in lap.
Daddy charcoaled meat on a tiny barbecue.

In the parlor, the grand piano was an animal with huge decaying teeth.
We thought the pedals could grab us like paws.

Sometimes Grandpa took us down to the basement's coal furnace.
Hard to believe the house sat over that dark pit.

At night I'd lie awake on the second floor, the street lamp outside
casting a pure arc of light onto the grass.

Something under the ground, under the dark pit,
almost spoke to me then.

I'd sit up straight, imagining hooves,
ladies in long dresses,

my mother and father turning over
restlessly in the room down the hall,

my brother beside me whimpering
like a small cat. Next smell would be toast,

my father's aftershave.
You going to dream all day?

Yes, I'd say. That's exactly what I'm going to do.
Who could explain what haunted me?

This is where Grandma lived
when she was a little girl.

How Deep Was the Silence There?

Deep as water
spun down a hole.

Seas colliding.
But clean, very clean.

Deep as birds calling us
to rise up any morning.

Brighter than we were.
Voices, in trees.

Peach. Melon sliced. Silence wider
than all mistakes.

Felt like a cake
they let you cut yourself.

Aziz, Under the St. Louis Arch

How can a refugee

stand under

a giant structure like that

and not feel hopeful?

Tomorrow, jackpot!

His little shop called World Gifts

would sell all its bronze vases

and Indian brocades

in one swoop.

The story he wrote for the

newspaper might win a prize.

Leaders of distant countries, shaking hands,

would invite him back

to run something, like a school,

or a government.

He dressed so carefully, smoothly shaved,
knotted tie, blip of cologne.

But this crying at home
was a mystery beyond measure.
You could walk under every shining gate,
not be able to escape.

Loving Ashley Bryan

I was four, cross-legged on the floor.
My mama sat beside me opening mail.

Her breath rose in a gasp.
She flew from gloom to joy.

Inside one thick envelope, a delicate hand-painted book,
crane on the cover. Thin white note, *This is for Naomi.*

But she wouldn't give it to me. She read the letter
in its perfect slanted script, then read it again.

Who is it from? I said. Can I hold it at least?
And she closed her eyes. She sighed.

I knew then there were secrets
we would live with all our lives, mysteries

no one could describe.
You make a friend, they change you forever.

But how do you tell someone else?

Later we would all know Ashley Bryan.

Like millions of other people in the world,

we would all fall in love with him, even my dad.

Every Sad Night

O little lost bedroom,
what was I thinking?
My mattress was slim,
the sheets felt cool.

What hopes,
imaginings
drifted through
a soft brown head
on a white pillow?

Important the closet door
had clicked.
Could not sleep
without that clicking.
So it couldn't open on its own.
No fears come
barging through.

I dreamed of a single beautiful boy

standing in a forest watching

everything but me.

Otto, Omus, Omar?

His name started with O.

He came, then he went.

The sorrow wraps around me

then and now

like a quilt.

What had I forgotten to say

that might have made him stay?

The Lie

My mother the beacon of honesty lied to me
only once. Dragged me to a beauty shop
for "a trim."

Behind my back, she must have motioned
Chop it all off. I came out gloomy
as a shaved Marine.

This was reason to be mad for a week,
to hide in my room, wear beanies pulled low,
to cry, to flail

and have a long braid or two
for the rest of my life.

Or a ponytail.

Freedom

My mother did not worry when I disappeared

on my blue bike,

biggest difference of the old days

versus the new.

Even bigger than internet and landline phones.

Back then, parents just let you go.

I'd glide on my wheels around old Ferguson,

soaking up houses, yards,

owning the blocks.

My friends and I threw our bikes down

in a grassy field.

We never locked them.

Played with sticks, fallen trees,

balls, the stones we stacked to make dams

in the creek.

No one got hurt except once

Marilyn jumped off her front porch

and a metal garden stake went through her body.

She survived, though.

Later she told us she would never be able

to have kids.

That sounded okay.

We didn't want kids.

⟡

My mom trusted us.

I'm not sure she trusted herself.

Each day I walked so fast

down the Harvey hill

toward our little house

with green shutters after school.

Was she still alive?

This was the bad secret I carried.

She might not be.

You could never tell your friends.

Before I was born, my mama tried to die.

I had to check on her.

Sometimes if I walked roundabout

through the big grassy field,

I'd see laundry flapping

from our backyard line
before I found her.
It seemed like a good sign.
Why would you wash
if you were planning to die?

Relieved at home, I curled in the corner,
read books, kept an eye out.

⚬⚬

When she locked herself in her room,
I could hear weeping. She didn't muffle it.
Sometimes she wailed like a scary coyote
in a cowboy movie.
I never knew what
made her cry. I never heard
anyone else's mother howl.
So I drifted around
outside her door,
kept offering tea.

⚬⚬

The mother likes to sleep. She might sleep all day
if you let her. But a tornado is coming. What
do we do before a tornado? Tie things down.

Fold up lawn chairs. Find the cat. We cowered

in our small hallway.

Only miles away a whole block was erased,

eaten by a tornado.

Hard to forget that.

        ⸘

No one ever said the word *depression*.

Maybe it wasn't invented yet.

Except for that time in history

when no one had any cash.

        ⸘

Holding her hand

before falling asleep

I focused on one prayer:

Let her hand

always be there.

Here, with me.

Don't let so much crying

make her die. Let her feel better.

I need her.

Outside

ancient pine trees

rustled and stretched

their waving fingers

in spooky shadows across my sill.

If she dies, could I still feel her grasp?

&

What will make the mother happy?

If you are a good girl? No.

That is not enough. What will be enough?

She has planted tulip bulbs along the street.

If they all come up, rows of yellow smiling cups

bright enough to make cars slow down,

will that be enough? If her father plants

two redbud trees? If my father gets home

earlier?

&

At the big art museum, in the hallway

of white marble arches, echoes welcome us.

People whisper across smooth air.

Polished floors. She lights up.

Her face lifts, eyes widened.

She never cries here.

Monet's lily pads make her calm.

She is always asking us questions.

What do you see? This one

speaks to me. These merging blues.

What speaks to you?

Brimming pools of color and shape.

Henry Moore sculptures help her mind

feel smooth. She cares nothing for armor,

portraits of dressy kings or queens. But the lemons

on a table next to a blue pitcher in Holland

a hundred years ago, yes!

The mother braiding her daughter's hair.

You don't have to like

anything best, she says. Just soak in the view,

hold it in your body. Where does it

take your brain?

         ❧

She never liked hanging up clothes.

They mounded in a chair,

piled like a story of previous days.

I would slide hangers

into the shoulders of Tuesday,

fold Wednesday's sweater,

clip Thursday's billowing skirt,

rescue crumpled Kleenexes

from every pants pocket,

place them on a table

by the bed. And I did this

forever. It's so crazy, life!

You don't know what your landmarks

are going to be. For me, a pile

of rumpled clothes

became a Mama holy place.

⬧

I went to church with her parents by myself

only once. Sat straight in the pew between them.

Kept hands in my lap, folded. Tried to sing

the hymns. My mom had told me,

You don't have to believe

anything you hear. But I liked it.

They all seemed

a little afraid.

⬧

Yes, she was fascinated by the Cahokia Mounds.

The tomb of Tutankhamun. The Swami Ramakrishna.

The holy Buddha. The child Mozart who wrote music age six.

The possibilities of reincarnation, transmigration—

she told me she had once been a butterfly.

At yoga school, I liked my mother in the child pose,

folded quietly.

She loved Peace Pilgrim, Gandhi, Adlai Stevenson, St. Francis.

She stood in the garden, her arms stretched to both sides.

I think she was waiting for something to land.

༄

Her handwriting sailed a straight sea. She shaped

cursive letters perfectly. Her lines knew there could be

peace on earth. Gregorian chants

behind chatter. Grace and dignity in a

sentence. *You need to practice.* Practice,

practice, practice. In the older days, everyone practiced

more. Never forget the old days were new days once.

Cursive meant connected. Flow. A sea of regular tides.

It was comforting to sit at its side.

༄

Why didn't she do what she was born to do?

Paint.

She was a prodigy! Everyone knew this!

Why did she stop? Why does anyone

stop doing their best thing?

I saw the evidence, paintings stacked

in my grandmother's bedroom. Paintings
leaning against the walls. Our house was filled
with her paintings. She was happiest
around paintings. So why? I didn't like
the way her face closed up when I asked.
The Fine Arts School at Washington University
gave her the first full scholarship
they ever gave any person on earth!
The great painter Max Beckmann said
she was his most *simpatico* student.
She didn't know the word,
had to look it up,
found it funny a German
used Spanish to describe.
The great painter Philip Guston said,
Your paintings are here
for me to enjoy. I offer no criticism.
These were her teachers,
they loved her.
They were famous artists!

Once she had a painting in an exhibition
and hers was the only one

that got stolen. This seemed

like a compliment.

She moved to Brooklyn.

She lived in a basement.

I lived in the dark.

∞

So what happened to her?

Her parents were tightly closed German boxes.

You couldn't get anything out of them

even if you fiddled with the latch all day.

Ask a question? They looked away.

I combed through her old drawers

in Grandma's bedroom. One silver bracelet engraved

with tipis and canoes. A cameo ring that fit no one.

The pale face without features could have been

a million women.

∞

We were interviewed by a Girl Scout lady

who promised to make me a leader.

My mother said, No! Please don't.

A follower would be preferred.

The lady said, A follower is a sheep!

My mom said, I want a sheep.

She wanted a sheep?

       ᘒ

My mom was so smart, she knew about food.

White bread, candy, soda pop, could kill you.

At age five I became a brown rice fresh vegetables yogini.

No dead animals for me, no carcass on my plate,

a chicken is a bird.

I carried dried apricots and almonds to Girl Scouts.

My friends didn't like it when treats were my turn.

Who could have guessed my mom would become

a junk food addict and later die of starvation?

I still cry when I pass a Dairy Queen.

       ᘒ

And yet, and yet

just in case, she collected

small rectangular tubs of grape jelly.

Her purse rustled with

slim salt and pepper envelopes

good in emergencies,

wrapped plasticware.

Once in a buffet line,

she stuck a green onion up her sleeve,

said she needed it for a recipe later.

We never stole things

never never never

but she gathered

what was offered,

small soaps from motels,

matchbooks,

took a few extra,

life was lean,

you never knew

one month to another

what might be needed.

You might be sitting

on a rock somewhere and

need a little jelly on your gloom.

       ॐ

A poem returns,

playing over and over in the mind.

I'm nobody nobody nobody,

it feels peaceful to be nobody.

No one can pin you down.

Little Farmer

With love to Molly Rockamann and Earthdance Farm

My mother pulled us up the hill in a red wagon.

We rolled home with brown sacks in our laps.

When I was twelve, I worked at Mueller's

Organic Farm, the rows knew my step.

I plucked berries gently, never bruising.

They paid five cents a box, it felt like a lot.

All my life has had that light, square shape.

Such ruddy sunstruck pride

in the farmers named Al and Caroline.

Al loved his mounds of squash, sacks of beans,

with fierce intensity. Caroline said, Nope, I only

love him. Their okra bore an essence of perfection,

ripe corn whispered inside its perfect sheaves

and drifty web of hair. You are here, it said.

You will always be here. Years later Al told me,

Your mother was the most lovely person

who ever walked up my drive, that long shiny

ponytail, those huge eyes. She asked

the best questions. That shows intelligence.

Al sang me songs, lost love and lonely stars.

Why didn't I ask more questions?

Our lives spin out. He wanted me to stay.

I wish I could harvest his patience

from fifty years away. Al long dead,

his dutiful Caroline dead, their farm still

a farm though, one victory! I'd tell him

how right he was about slowness,

the path of sunlight through leaves,

how dirt has always befriended me,

birdcalls beyond,

how his shy smile, waving goodbye with a hoe,

stayed with me forever, how no tomato

was ever better than the one he held in his hand.

Menagerie

She let me have
a chicken,
then a rooster.

She let me have a mouse,
then a rat.

Each evening I held Ralph,
the rat, stroking his white head,
while my parents watched
the evening news. I tickled
his tiny pink ears.

My father disliked all this
so much.
He could not feel comfortable
if a rat was in the room.
He could not understand
the New World.

Out

No one is big enough to notice
all that might be noticed.

No one is small enough,
no one is big enough.

Distraction, a shaggy dog
in the center of days
always needing to go out.

A child's job is to soak up details,
crawl around rooms,
move little things,
touch.

A child's job is to stare.
When speaking comes around,
to take that *why* and use it,
apply to everything,
not let big people off the hook.

Many big people deserve the hook.
All big people who do not put lives
of children and teenagers first
should be
removed from power.
OUT.

Messy

To have the word MESSY in bold
under one's picture
in a high school yearbook
might mark a life, right?

She shrugged.
Said she didn't care.

Mom! How could you not care?
Most beautiful
Most likely to succeed
marked the photos
of your friends, but
you got MESSY?

Were they your enemies,
the yearbook editors?
Did they apologize?

She shrugged again.

I had no enemies.

I don't remember anything about it.

And later to learn that Tennessee Williams

attended her same high school!

Mom! Why didn't you tell me?

We weren't there at the same time.

Your teacher Philip Guston

taught his students

to look for light from multiple sources.

Maybe you knew *MESSY*

was only one angle.

Broken Season

The fountain is broken.
The swing set is broken.
Even the silver trash can
sports a charred hole
through the bottom
from the time
Daddy decided
to burn the trash.
And the broken-handled bucket
for water, for dirt, for sand,
oh, I loved that bucket.

When a family enters an era
of brokenness,
things will change.

Doors slam hard.
Doors sound broken.

The child is no longer
a child for a while.

Sex Education

After hearing my auntie
couldn't have a baby
because of her husband,
I felt confused.
What did Uncle have to do with it?
I asked my mother,
who gave me a bright orange book
about pollen called *Big Me, Little Me.*

The story meandered through
a garden, flowers, stems,
honeybees hovering
in cups of petals,
confusing my brain.
Mom, what is this?

I was asking about people, not bees.
She stared at me ominously.
There is so much you do not know.

And that was all she ever said

on the subject.

She handed me a hose,

a little shovel.

She sent me to the berry patch

with a silver bowl.

Elsewhere

"No matter how far the town, there is another beyond it."

—Proverb from Mali

Always we were imagining others,

the ones who slept when we woke

and woke when we slept.

We were calling out to the far towns,

hoping they found enough food,

their bowls were filled with fruit.

Hoping the night air held them gently, too.

Did we ever think of you enough, far town?

Were we able to imagine your rivers,

your pain? Did you sometimes feel

the world forgot you?

You were the world

as much as we were.

Flashbulb

The *St. Louis Post-Dispatch* used to feature recipes
from locals in the Sunday magazine, one a week,
large color photographs presenting the chef like
a movie star. Daddy in starched white shirt
with rolled-up sleeves was making his famous
hummus. Hummus was still exotic then, not stocked
in every grocery store in the USA. Photographers
arrived, set up elaborate lighting, my father stirred and smashed
his garbanzos, my mother presented the chopped garlic clove
gently as an aide in a surgical unit, he squeezed the lemon,
drizzled the olive oil, grilled the pine nuts, they were both interviewed.
Hail the lovely hummus! We sat in the corner,
out of camera view, hungry.
The moment the interview session finished,
hummus sitting like a giant flower on a round plate
in the center of the fresh tablecloth,
decorated with olives, griddled onions, and sumac
in Daddy's special way, we heard a loud pop. Small slivers of glass
scattered everywhere. Bright sharp daggers on our bare arms,
littering the tablecloth, and worst of all, the hummus.
The photographer yelled.

His flashbulb had never exploded before.

We brushed each other off.

My mama had glass in her hair.

Many apologies, the man departed,

glad he'd finished his work before this happened.

My father walked sadly

with his masterpiece toward the trash can

to throw it away. No one could eat it now.

My mother cried, saying she could scrape off the top.

I walked to my room and lay down, musing

on how swiftly moods change and once again,

photography was dangerous.

Every Age

If you open the door

to happiness

what comes through?

Friends come through.

Something new comes through.

Something you never did before

and might do

seems easy.

Something familiar

carries new spark.

Seeds cradled in a hand.

Fresh T-shirts folded

into smooth color-coded stacks.

Smelling the breeze they held

on the clothesline.

Carrying cookies to the unknown family

who just moved in down the block.

Meeting the mom.

Knowing Norma Jean's mother

was always in her dining room sewing,

whatever the weather,

little needle working hard,

pumping up and down,

thread bobbin spinning,

and what dresses emerged,

pastel dresses with collars and ruffles,

was a chord connecting the days.

Norma Jean gave me her old dresses

when she got new ones. She was taller

and plumper, my mom could

tighten the seams.

I feared nothing I gave

could ever be enough.

No math paper with 100 branded in red,

no pint box of blackberries

picked that morning

by my bumbling hand,

birthdays and Christmases

gave me panic attacks.

Is it possible

to be every age at once,

forever?

Some say so.

Leave the door open.

Shopping with Parents

The Indian trader perched among split lentils and almonds.
The Lebanese vendor endlessly arranged his necklaces and breads.
There were hours when nobody came.

We entered exotic markets, tipsy little shops, lost bazaars.
My parents had an instinct for underdogs, back road bakeries.
We stopped everywhere that was Going Out of Business.

Baskets, bargains, cut-out bins, clearances. Two for One.
We hovered in a crooked spice shop somewhere, coats smelling
of cinnamon for days. Chicago, Des Moines,

Decatur, and later Tampico, London, Lisbon,
my parents had a knack for grandmas sitting with quilts,
immigrants weighing homemade noodles at the Italian depot.

No new strip centers for us. No malls or flashy big box stores.
Here we are at our favorite destination, an abandoned-looking
warehouse between two mounds of dust.

I swear I once spent an entire month in a Jerusalem falafel stall

with my dad. He was learning the whole process perfectly by heart

and taste testing each morsel. Then we paused at a bookstore

where they were selling

every book he ever read in his life in both languages.

He wanted to read them all again.

Beacon

1.
Children who live in sad houses
hope to fix them.

Like a bulldozer in a bedroom,
that heavy.

If there is a thread,
children are always reaching for it,

nothing but tangles
knotting, with spaces between.

I'd rather
knit a hat.

Moods are so
hard to predict.

Let's start over.
Let's solve just this one thing.

Don't worry so much—
the least helpful advice in the world.

A kitchen feels like a cage.

2.
Some days,
school could be relief.

The teacher sent her little students
to the front of the room, saying,

You will speak without mumbling
and never swallow the end of a line.

She believed in you
before you did.

Calmly she sat, hands folded,
golden bracelets glistening with light

that fell exactly
onto the middle of her desk.

As she would dwell forever
in the middle of your mind,

listening
for a lifetime.

There might be a stage and you could stand on it.
Really? Corners of bookstores,

basements of libraries, someone might come to listen.
Really? Someone believed you could.

Duets

My mother's strong hands
on the keyboard
were a comfort zone.

I sat on her left,
always playing the lower notes.

There was no sadness
at the keys.
Only a pilgrimage toward calm.

There we go! she'd say,
making it through a difficult passage.
Or *Ahhhhh*, at the end of a piece
we knew well.

Sometimes we played a page
over and over
to polish its heart.

We loved "The Lost Chord"
and tried to find it for many years.

Pizzicato possibilities,

arpeggio challenges,

staccato surprise,

grace note riffs, the language

of music, I wanted an

andante day.

As a little girl, she taught herself to play

when her father wouldn't let her take lessons.

Made a long paper keyboard out of cardboard,

on her floor. She read a book

from the library to learn.

               Wasn't that hard?

It was all hard.

               How could you learn

               if you couldn't even hear it?

Beethoven went deaf.

               Right, but he already knew how to play.

She said there was always a way.

How Will the Child Ever Leave This House?

The child will not leave.
The child will be wearing this roof as a hat forever.

This house will be sitting like the lion at the zoo in the corner
of his compound, eyes on you.

It's probably not you he's really considering.
Perhaps the shadowy movements that

trapped him here, the nets or lassoes or stun guns,
things you know nothing of. But you're shaped like

the strange forces who did it to him.
He can't imagine what you, or anyone like you, might do next.

Locusts' Lament

I love the one you might have been.

You love the me that reminds you of yourself.

Stop telling me what to do, you said.

I birthed you. That's my position.

⚮

Once a vine came through

my mother's bedroom window

and wrapped around her head

in the dark, like a crown.

In the morning she raised her hand

to touch it, and screamed.

What did you do to me?

she said.

We were innocent as the locusts

droning toward sundown.

Pure as the puffy clouds

drifting over the river

which never gave a secret away

and never stayed.

The Pleaser

I tried so hard, it was pitiful.
What was I wanting?
To fix things. Fix anything.
She said, Don't write about me.
Write about your dad,
the frozen cat,
your friend who moved
back to Canada. Describe
those cream puffs you made
such a big deal about.

So I hid what I did.
Notebooks in shoeboxes
dusty under the bed.
Didn't write about her, though.

Why do we need someone to say
you make me happy,
you're great.
Is that a basic need
like sleeping and eating?

I struggled, I tried.
When the teacher said
I carried the devil within me,
she cried for a week.

Trust me, it's true.
Exact quote.
I just found the report card.
My mother saved it all these years.
She also saved my ten thousand
notes and letters
saying I loved her so much.

Also pages she wrote to herself
declaring how nice I was.
A stellar daughter
who would do anything for her, you bet.

Yet. It must have been harder
when she was younger
to say so.

Living in Jerusalem

After my parents divorced and remarried
within three months,

moving to Jerusalem, my father's hometown,
didn't seem that dramatic.

They never talked about this later.
So many things people never talk about!

Before we moved, they got rid of almost everything
except the ancestral red Magic Chef stove

which they parked in a barn. I have no memory
how they did that. Where did everything go?

And how can it be I ended up with tubs of ancient papers
and letters and photographs at this late date?

My mother, in Jerusalem, applied to work
at the BBC radio station because

my father had worked there as a boy.
A shy person who hadn't spoken in public much,

suddenly my mother was on the radio,
discussing culture, interviewing people, being a DJ!

Anemic, she required daily iron shots administered
by her teenaged daughter with no medical training.

I have talked a lot about our crazy lives in Jerusalem,
but less about my mother there and she

was probably the bravest one of all.
When we had to flee a war, carrying nearly nothing again,

she looked around those rooms we had furnished from scratch,
red brocade pillow against handmade cotton sofa cushions,

woolly sheep blankets, beds, simple kitchen shelves,
and said softly, I hope someone nice finds you

and can use you.

Life Decision

Sometimes a life decision is made in the middle

of the Atlantic Ocean on a famous ship's second-to-last run.

You and your family stumbled onto the Queen Mary

in south England, knowing it was going to New York,

but not where you would go once you got there.

Other travelers having canceled, your dad bought tickets

with less than four days' notice. Our cabin was not prime.

In those days, boats cranked out newspapers daily,

telling passengers what was happening in the wider world.

I, who could barely grasp the immediate world,

listened closely at the breakfast table

as our parents discussed the disaster in Jerusalem,

places we might live. On Wednesday,

a news story popped up about San Antonio.

Voted *Cleanest City in the USA* that year (which seems

astonishing, having now picked up trash here for decades),

my parents thought it might be a choice.

San Antonio was preparing for a big global fair

and we were . . . global.

So what did we think?

Two kids eating strawberries on pancakes,

we shrugged, both said, Fine, great, Texas?

Good, should be warm. Let's go someplace warm.

War felt cold.

My father folded the newspaper carefully,

as if it were a piece of lace,

placed it next to his coffee cup,

said, Texas, here we come.

My parents had no jobs or home waiting in Texas.

Once my father had given directions

to an evangelical preacher from Texas in Jerusalem,

but that was the extent of our connection. And look.

I'm still here.

Texas

The days were so hot you could walk out of your house
and disappear. Return as a puff of smoke.
Blooming vines shriveled on a fence while
you were gone. I loved the old raggedy streets,
lost edges of time, oddities, *World's Largest Pecan*
proudly inhabiting Seguin's town square. There weren't
as many people, guns, or human nuts back then. Not as many
flags or fanatics. But I do recall the church where people
spoke in tongues, waved their arms, screamed *Jehovah!*
then later asked my dad in a normal voice if he wanted
to grab a bite.

My parents bought the first house they looked at.
Of course they did. This was how they rolled,
though they thought Holy Rollers were extreme.
They didn't pass a lot of judgment though. Women
held hands in our living room. My pals talked to my dad
about pot. I wouldn't touch pot or take an aspirin.
A bit Amish by nature, I absorbed *The Whole Earth Catalog,*
planned a tipi, sewed a quilt. Texas had room for
everyone back then, and it seemed important to pronounce
Blanco Road correctly.

On the Couch

Never ask your mother
what she's been
doing all day
when you're a grumpy teenager
and come home to find her
lying on the couch.

Hi Mom!
Algebra is killing me!
What have you been doing all day?
Watching TV?

She jumped up,
furious.

My life is constant labor!
You have no idea!
Endless chores!
Who is this rude girl
living in our home?

Teaching Yourself

I played the piano,
taught by my mom,
then
the violin.

Second chair
youth orchestra violin,
taught by a disheveled genius,
then
the drums.

Lots and lots of lessons.
Drum lessons in a dank basement
with a tough lady. Padded walls.
I wanted to play tympani
in a symphony.

Drum lessons cost three dollars

for thirty minutes.

I played bass drum

in a marching band

one semester only,

kicked out

for misplaced booms.

Drums,

then

the guitar.

The guitar, I taught myself.

And it's the only thing

I still play.

Lost Kids

Armor is *amor*
with an extra *r*.
We need a lot of *amor*
as armor in this life
otherwise we might
crumple. Whatever mood
they were in, we never questioned
our parents' love. At least, I didn't.
My father started buying land
whenever he could, refugees want a place
to sink a root. He bought ugly land,
off-the-beaten trail land, cheap land,
scrubby snaky land in places like Stockdale.
He bought fifty acres and acted ranchy,
stood on a stoop in his boots, saying, This will be yours someday.
Please Dad, no. I said. I'm Amish, but I don't want land. Coyotes
killed his goat. They ate his chickens. He let rotten gazebos stay
rotten. Pears fell.

ॐ

My parents were famous for "losing us." They'd walk ten steps ahead
in a store, on a street, in a town where we'd never been. They lost me

in Portugal at a loud carnival. A terrifying clown tried to kiss me.

They lost me in Fairbanks, Alaska, for three hours.

I didn't mind going places by myself which was better

than going with them and ending up lost.

Were they exhausted? Did they need

a little time to themselves? Once

I found them sitting on a bench

behind a giant hedge

in Forest Park

in the snow

holding

hands.

What Was the Secret in Your House?

Some fight, some crack the whip.

Some leave a gun lying on a table.

Some never come home when they say they will.

Some spend a lot of time looking in a mirror.

His parents had to have their beer.

Her brother locked her in the garage

with his motorcycle.

Her daddy insulted the girls

but never the boys.

Is there always a secret?

My mom cried and I didn't want people to know.

My friend hid the fact her mom

didn't speak English well.

But sometimes it's a good secret, maybe?

They love you more than they can ever say?

What Next

Once we drove home to San Antonio from Nuevo Laredo
with an eight-year-old named Alberto in our car.

He wore stenciled brown cowboy boots,
a red plaid shirt. No luggage. The boy's father,

who owned the motel where we had stayed,
was asking for a small favor. Could we bring his son

to American elementary school for five months
to learn English? Even then, this sounded

like human trafficking, sheer insanity.
Could he stay with us? Unbelievably,

my parents said yes. Important detail:
they did not know this man.

But they always wanted to help. Did he have
a passport? Was it even legal?

I recall arguing furiously with them
in the seedy motel room. My mom said,

You took Spanish in middle school.
You can talk to him most.

I didn't want to remind her
I had also studied Arabic and German.

Time has swallowed facts.
The man could have disappeared forever,

given a false name, anything. He promised
to pick the boy up next summer.

How did we cross the border?
What was wrong with my parents?

Back home
they set up a cot in my room.

It was hard to explain this to
friends and neighbors.

Alberto always wore his cowboy boots.
I walked him home from school.

How did we spend our evenings?
Did he ever utter an English word?

I recall him holding my hand,
cot to bed, whimpering like a small cat

in the dark. What children are forced
to endure!

The next June we were out in the front yard,
laughing, blasting each other with the hose,

when very slowly
his dad rolled up.

Homicide Channel

You'd sit spellbound, serious,
wrapped in a blanket,
curled inside a terrible tale,
munching popcorn.

Mom!

It's like a puzzle to me, you said.
I try to figure it out before they do.
It's not a bad thing. Stop
bugging me.

Mom!

You didn't find it scary to imagine
the terrible things a human might do.
When I was little, and TVs first came
into houses, boxy animals with four legs,

you banned me from watching a mouse
that could fly. Mighty Mouse.
My friends liked him so I wanted
to know him, too.

He will give you bad dreams, you said.
You must keep your mind clean.

History of Getting Older

Once long ago
I was you
and you were
nowhere.

Really?

Once we had no teeth.
Our gums were smooth
as ice.

Later you bit
your own finger
and cried.

A story went inside
and pulled us out
like a bouquet.

Listen to this!
It happened!

After days that said
Maybe and *If*
came one brave day
that said
At last.
You went to school.
You tied your own shoes.

The future embraced
by the wavery past.

Waiting for Morning

"I always wait for the morning, but don't know why
the morning never comes."

                    —*Sitti, 103 years old*

My Palestinian grandma who prayed five times a day,
even her devotion couldn't bring the morning
bigger than sunshine.

Was she waiting for roads to open,
blockades to disappear,
flurries of almond blossoms
showering upon the road?

Turn left to Ramallah,
then south to Jerusalem.
Tear gas was not her language.
When gassed in her own room
by soldiers in uniform, she said to me
in Arabic, Never mind. They're lost.

She wanted to find her old house
still murmuring her name
in its wrought-iron handrail,
broad stairs shining.
The rooms she never wanted to leave
still gleaming in the light.

"Keep Up Your Joyous Practices"

My mom saved letters for fifty years
addressing her as
Dearest Immortal Self.

Devotees welcomed her
to sacred communities,
urged her to stay strong

in yogic devotion.
Don't miss a day.
Soon she would be a great sage

radiating forth
as blessed sunbeam!
Even during broken times,

my mother's hope girded her life.
I don't think she ever visited
the cosmic Connecticut
commune, though.

I did. It wasn't fun.
The Zen Buddhists of California
won her heart forever, though,
surrounding her with silence,

books, food. She felt accepted
without question. Same with the Presbyterians
of Texas. Maybe it's all we ever want.

Acceptance without question.

&

Silence says
I live here
even when you don't.

Don't worry,
I hold your place open.

If you try to take me away,
you'll lose me.
I'll fall out of your satchel
when the car climbs that ridge.

Just leave me here,

poke these little cones of emptiness

into your coming days.

They'll grow, you know.

I promise.

Titanic Daddy

On the day of your death
nine years later
a key will be sold
from a locker on
the most famous ship
that ever sank.

It is called
exceptionally rare
as you also were
and belonged to a steward
named Sidney.

His family kept the key
when his body was recovered
from the wreckage.
Many people would give
a lot of money
for this key now
though it opens nothing
on their ground.

You kept the keys
to your lost Jerusalem home
lonely keys since 1948
heavy keys too big for a pocket.

You kept turning them
on a desk
a shelf
dusting them off
to help you tell your story.

Beach

The mother washes over us
like a wave.
When she is calm
all the seabirds
dip and soar,
cormorants bask
on a lip of breeze,
one egret balances.

When she is rough
you say, I'd do anything
to calm you.
Run on the beach,
scarf flapping,
hair tangled,
calling for help, or clues.
Wildly,
    worriedly,
        desperately.

I'd do anything for you.

And I did.

The mother is a coastal preserve.

Protect her.

Everything Planted Was a Calm

Billowing mint, basil, Mexican sunflowers
with nine-foot stalks, a tiny orange bloom.
White roses in a pot.
Daddy's fig tree
netted against the birds.
Iris bulbs, a hand shovel.

One year you grew a garden
in a neighbor's yard.
She had better light, fewer trees.
I asked if you had gotten
her permission.

At sundown you crossed through
the broken fence to water it. I remember
seeing you from the kitchen window,
hose held high, spray cascading,
and smiling, when you hadn't
smiled all day.

PART TWO

Sometimes We Need
a Bigger Family

Nina

Ever elegant.

Fine clothes, perfect hair.

You stirred care in every room.

Gentle, hopeful, positive.

Beautiful furniture.

Tabletops shining.

Classic burgundy rugs.

Food on the stove.

Just come visit me whenever you can.

Mass every day.

You loved to pray.

You prayed for us.

You prayed for everyone.

We felt comfort

in your radius.

Evelyn

She said, If you come by, I'll make you a peach pie.
But you have to tell me when you're coming.
No more of this drop-in stuff!
Peach pie takes gathering,
patience,
slow ripening first.

Evelyn lived in Cyclone, Texas,
but wasn't rattled.
Even raising eleven children,
she seemed calm.
They helped raise each other.
Later I missed one of her daughters
who had moved to Australia and said,
I'm sure you do, too.

She shook her head vigorously.

I don't have to!

I know her so well,

she's with me all the time.

If you know someone well

enough, you don't

ever have to miss them.

This is good advice.

It can really help you in this life.

Dorothy

Before someone visited,
she arranged tiny vases
of larkspur, nasturtium,
at the guest bedside.

The petals whispered,
This house is
ready for you.
We are welcoming you
in the quietest ways.

Helene

Helene told us we wouldn't love Thoreau very long.
He was a youthful crush, teenagers dreaming of simple lives

but soon, in our quest for grown-up stability, fancy houses,
sleek cars, pendulum lighting,
wineglasses, wardrobes, and stiff hair like hers,

we'd give him up. Her daughter and I stared at each other grumpily
as she rushed back and forth to the table with fancy salads.

It was difficult to argue with other people's parental
convictions back then. I can tell her now.

She was wrong.

Odette

Come see me if you can.
You don't have to come, it's too much effort.

We can just eat here.
I'd love to go out and get some Mexican food.

I wish my girl lived closer.
It's great she's following her dreams in her life.

I don't really want to stick around much longer.
Isn't this a terrific big apartment?

And what about the mothers who . . .

hurt.

Abused.

Accepted what the fathers did

even if it was cruel,

horrific.

And didn't tell.

Didn't support their daughters.

There were those mothers, too.

Picture:

A counselor's office in a Texas school.

I am telling two middle-aged women

what is happening to my friend

in her home.

They call her a liar. Call me a liar, too.

Tell me never to come back.

They stand in the doorway of their office

as I leave.

Get out, you bad tattler. No parents

could ever do

what you say.

So then—

she ran away.

And she never saw her parents again.

But we found each other

years later, and she was still a gentle person,

having not been listened to,

who felt it hard to do much

in this world.

Green Shirt

His mother did not wash it for this,
for him to be carried dead by two friends
across the thirsty ground of Gaza.

That morning he put it on, she told him
he looked handsome, a fine deep color
that lit up his skin.

Marilyn #1

My mom's best friend wrote a poem
about a wide-eyed doll she saved.
I carried the poem with me for years,
comforted by someone else's nostalgia.
She shaped perfect poems about rocks
and trees and time. She kept crayon pictures
on her refrigerator after people were grown.
Little landmarks everywhere.
In her final years I visited her in a care home.
Her whole bed was covered with dolls.

Marilyn #2

The most joyous mom I ever met.
Friends with Mr. Rogers.
He lived in her NEIGHBORHOOD,
knocked on her back door,
her youngest son fainted to see him there.
She had seven kids, maybe people
with a lot of kids have more practice.
She wrote tiny poems in tiny books.
Laughed at everything.
Made my son popcorn for breakfast
when he requested it. He was two.
When she asked him what he liked
to drink with breakfast,
he said, *How about a little wine?*
She told this story for years.

Crying Monkey

A boy with his grandma sat across

the airplane aisle from my son and me.

The boy fingered his window shade, sliding it up and down.

Grandma slapped his hand.

Don't touch that!

My son whispered, Why can't he touch that?

The boy gripped a monkey toy in his other hand.

He saw us staring and held his monkey out to us, smiling.

Hand-knitted gray wool, grimacing plastic stitched-on head,

three large blue hand-painted tears.

The monkey wore a red knitted beanie,

which the boy pulled down

over its eyes, then laughed.

Grandma pointed at it. Isn't that the ugliest thing

you've ever seen?

It's ridiculous. He won't leave it at home.

The boy rocked the monkey tenderly.

I said, I think it's cute.

Grandma said, His mama died last July.

I've been keeping him. His daddy hasn't shown up

since he was a baby.

My son was reaching toward the monkey,

the boy handed it across the aisle.

The monkey had plastic hands and feet like a human.

My son wagged them around, made them clap.

He clapped one hand with one foot.

Both boys laughed.

Then the woman on my other side

spoke for the first time, as if just awakening.

I'm on my way to east Texas to visit my son in prison.

The only thing that keeps me going is remembering

other prisoners have mothers, too

who must feel as bad as I do.

She looked at the monkey.

That really is the worst toy I ever saw, she said.

My son handed it back to the boy,

who hugged it hard and closed his eyes.

Not-Yet-Mother

She saved things.

Vintage bib, miniature yellow cotton socks.

Getting ready for another life,

down the path of someday,

in the grand better box of someday

that floated above calendars

and schedules. There would be a morning

of nothing but birdsong in that place

and a small person waking up

to listen with her.

Forgive Us

Neon the turtle
laid six eggs
in her red backyard tub.
For sixteen years
we had called her a "he."

The eggs couldn't hatch
since she had no friends but us.
Then she sneaked through the gate
a plumber left open.

To jump in the river, we hoped.
Hopefully she could get there,
only a block and a half,
a biologist said a turtle would be
able to smell river water,
I hope so,
we never saw her again.

Sixteen years
is a long time
to tend a turtle.
We missed her
more than we ever
could have dreamed.
Her watchful eye
from the corner of the yard
under a shady tree
that died after she left.
Even when she'd hibernate
for months,
disappearing under a shed,
we missed her.

She wasn't slow.
She liked orange foods
and the yellow blossom
esperanza, hope.

We never knew
where she made her secret bed.

Write a seven-word autobiography right now

Addicted to simplicity
from very first day.

Ever hopeful, ever growing
always asking why.

So many places
we haven't seen yet.

The space around the poem
is best.

Shatzie at Her Ranch

She could be anywhere.
In the far pasture,
in a dream.

We think she crossed a field
with her silver bucket
toward the cluster of weeds.

She may have gone into town
if someone picked her up.
But what would she be wanting?

Might she be wandering
the dry creek bed with cows,
their swollen bellies, drizzling snouts?

She did not leave a message.
The clouds know where she goes.
Little curly worms under sago palms.

Screen door.
The gate left open.

Wild Card

1

Reprise of details: my mom married

the first Arab she ever met,

three months after meeting him.

They married in a friend's living room in Topeka,

where neither of them really lived.

Aziz invited the governor of Kansas to their wedding

(he didn't come) and the president of the local bank

(he came). My mother's parents, who only trusted

Lutherans, were furious, so wouldn't attend the wedding.

My parents-to-be followed their hearts, their dreams.

Seems reckless to me.

2

My high school friends and I
told our parents we were going
to a movie, but another movie
in the next theater,
Valley of the Dolls,
had a better poster,
so we saw it instead.
I closed my ears for bad
language. My parents never used
bad language, so I felt shocked.
Covered my eyes
for racy naked scenes.
Back home my mom asked
for details about the movie
and I dropped a new bottle of
ketchup on the floor.
Red mess splattered half the kitchen.
It was fine, I stuttered.
Instantly she knew I lied.
What movie did you really see?
My father said,
Did you even go to the movies?

They were detectives, could pick up any clue.

I told them.

I also mentioned I hated it.

They blew up.

I couldn't go anywhere

for a week.

You are such a *wild card*, my mother said.

It's Sunday and Everyone Is Hungry

Silver saucepans lined up, measuring cups.

Nothing is instant then.

No microwave, no pre-made.

Starting from scratch took planning,

still does, always will.

What are you hungry for?

Peace on the planet.

A fruit plate, ringing a mound

of cottage cheese.

A bowl of crackers,

a sliced apple.

Nothing fancy,

it would make her cry.

Let's just go out.

Mama Counsel

Never wear red with black.
It's bad luck.

Never sleep on your left side
after eating or your food won't digest.

Prayer doesn't change things.
You do. Speak the words.

Hair spray is toxic!
Life is too beautiful to give up hope.

Someday we'll all figure out
what everything was for.

Life is a test.
What are we supposed to learn?

You just have to remember to write
your thank-you letters on your own.

Beans and corn make perfect protein
when eaten together.

She studied reflexology with a Chinese healer
and cured a swami's three-day hiccups

with a foot massage. Nerve endings
live in every part of your body!

She refused to quit her ill-begotten job
in a porno bakery she hated

because *It's good to finish*
what you start. Even if you didn't realize

what you were
starting.

Oh hail! And she loved
being served. A china teacup on a silver tray

was heaven to her! Glory hallelujah!
Tea at 4 p.m. is civilized, like the Queen!

I could stumble through my days and
never find a greater joy.

Growing Up

We won't move out,
  so our parents do.
My brother and I stay
    in their old house
  two more years.

When our parents drive away
  I wave and wave
until their car
  is smaller than my hand.

Guinea Pig

My mother and her friends wished to visit
the clairvoyant they'd heard about.
So they sent me to test her out.

A humble wooden home, on a street named for a tree.
I didn't drive yet. I asked my friend to drive me.
This was not a new thing for my mother.

She'd also sent me to the Hindu breathing swami,
the Filipino faith healers.
Always first, as her personal guinea pig.

My friend waited in the darkened living room.
I was escorted to another parlor by a man
in a sleeveless undershirt, then seated in a chair.

The clairvoyant, who charged five dollars, said,
"I'd like to talk about your friend out there."

"Yes?" She was a plump woman in a printed dress.

"Her mother just died and she's grieving terribly.
She was asked to drive her mother
across the border for treatment, and it didn't work. Tell her she did

everything she could. Her mother is fine. Her mother is with her
all the time. You must promise to tell her
the moment you leave. Right now, she has

many more problems than you." I was stunned. The facts
of this were true. She stared at me somewhat disinterestedly.
"I see books coming out of your hands. What does this mean?

Do you love books? I see your grandmother across the
ocean in a long dress. She can't read and she
loves you very much. Take time for her. She's important.

And don't marry that professor everyone likes.
Something's not right about him.
You'll find your way."

An hour of details later, I staggered back to the living room,

notes I scribbled gripped in my hand,

to find my friend nearly comatose on the couch.

I told her the moment we drove away. "This is good news!

Your mother is here!" My friend dropped out

of college after that freshman year and has let

the angels guide her all her life.

Everyone

1.

When my mother was a little girl at recess,
her teacher told her to run to the office for help.
I think I'm dying, she said.
My mother ran, conveyed the terrible message.
Don't you ever say such a bad thing again!
the school secretary shouted. A nurse rushed
to the playground to find the teacher on the ground
under the swings, dead.

My mom loved that teacher so much.
She threw up, felt sick for days,
couldn't return to school.
To carry such a hard message,
then be yelled at . . .

Everyone has burdens.

2.

My mom became a Montessori teacher
who loved three-year-olds best of all.
Her giant handmade flashcards of numbers
and letters crowded our tables.
The *A* was ten inches tall.
The *M* a mountainous landscape.
She loved helping three-year-olds pour rice
into measuring cups
and be neat. She wasn't neat at all but
she liked helping them be neat.

Everything is a mystery.

3.

Once my mom wept
outside a Dallas ballet,
angry I had taken her there,
saying she'd always wished
to be a ballet dancer as a child,
with her own teacher,
pink tutu, shoes.

Her father said ballet
was too expensive,
she wasn't strong enough.

How could this be?
She'd carried a dream
but never mentioned it to me.

We drove home silently,
not even discussing
the great performance.

Everyone has secrets.

Mom's Poem to Dandelions in the Land of the Midnight Sun, Alaska

(Secret poems she scribbled everywhere)

Just yesterday you were a field of
proud yellow blooms

Today a field of gossamer full moons

That Time When Everything Was Scotland

I'd gaze down from a high turret window

to see you trudging among sheep, bunnies,

a grim expression on your face.

How could anyone be sad in the most gorgeous

place on earth, the Isle of Mull? We were staying in

a castle. Never easy to explain a mood

to someone who wasn't feeling it, too.

A friend had hauled our suitcases

up the steep stairs as if we were both

old ladies already. Teatimes, lavishly

packed with scones and butters and jams.

I thought I could stay there

among hedgehogs and hedgerows

forever, happily, needing nothing

from a city ever again,

but you, such a gloomy mystery you were,

your colony of sorrows ruled by a

mysterious queen no one could see.

My mom's hunger for news

To know what was going on
be tuned in
caring about displaced children
needing safe homes in
war zones
hungry on street corners

She sent money to
teenaged boys in Houston
Indians in the Dakotas
toddlers in Gaza
This meant she was
everyone's grandma
to the tune of fifteen bucks
or maybe ten

Dozing with Mute on
every day a terrible ribbon of happenings
flashing across bottom of the screen
What could she do?
How could she care?

The charities remembered her

They sent so many begging letters

stacks that felt personal

She was still part of humanity

They kept her in touch

My Mom Serves Tea to Her Robbers

Later she will say, they wore white shirts,
their faces were kind. One took milk and sugar in his tea.

They had an interest in how she'd been living alone,
in that long brick house, since my father died.

How brave! They'd noticed the crack in her driveway, and
said she would soon be arrested by the city of Dallas

if she didn't give them twelve thousand dollars
to fix it. They were sitting at her kitchen table, smiling.

One was so handsome you wouldn't believe.
I'm sure they were handsome, Mom, that's probably

how they're able to con. She left two in her house and drove
the shortest one to the bank, where she extracted

the cash. He was quite visible in the security film. She felt cared for.
She was so happy they were going to save her

from the city of Dallas which, till that day,
had always been her friend.

Since when are you scared of the city of Dallas, but not of three strange men?
Later, it was impossible to reason with her.

Huff. She remained lucid, generally, except for this frolic,
this boisterous tête-à-tête, her pricey poor choice.

Years Later

I saw a headline in a magazine.
DOES DEPRESSION HOLD YOU
BACK FROM WHAT YOU ENJOY?

I thought, sure does.
And it's not even my depression.

I understand why "press" is in that word,
it's a pressure clamping from all sides,
floating in air, can't find its source
or brush it away. It's the armor we
never liked at the museum,
heavy and clanky.

So much energy spent
trying to solve it.
What did we do wrong?

When the lows finally left her,
she felt a fuse blowing out.
Everything exploded,
cracking and sparking.
For two weeks she talked gibberish,
said every nurse at the hospital
was my biological sister . . .
those days scared me. Life had
ignited, beyond our control.

Then her light grew calm forever.
She slept a month and woke up
lucid, cheerful. Stayed that way for
nine more years.

What a mystery!
Even her psychiatrist
was baffled. Depression
dissolved.

Taj Mahal

After years of anticipating
the world's most beloved building,
regal white sheen, elaborate profile,
my mother felt giddy in her Indian taxi.
She and her driver approached Agra to find
the roadway totally blocked.
The driver threw up his hands.
No, madam! This does not happen!
This cannot happen to us today!
He leapt from the car to inquire.

My mother would remember staring out
across muddy fields, a lone donkey, resting plow,
slow drift of thick clouds in the sky.
The day felt bright and hopeful but
it seemed an American politician
famous for declaring war
had taken over the whole city that day,
demanding security,
every road to Agra blocked,
not for an hour, not for two,

but for twenty-four.

And we were flying away.

That evening she sighed, saying,

Ah well, I've imagined it

all my life, I can keep imagining.

Maybe anticipating

was the greatest thing.

I saw a child with a balloon.

I saw a donkey.

As she drifted off to sleep,

she wondered out loud,

But what does it feel like to be so hated

no one else may enter a whole city

on the day that you do?

A Great-Grandma

When the fourth generation came to be with us,
time became a circle. No straight lines.
You both needed milk, naps.
He dropped a pita chip.
A red bird flew away with it.
You laughed.

So much joy
gathered around one person,
who he might become,
how he might
unfold.

A little girl handed him
a yellow leaf from the sidewalk.
He held it gently, stared at it,
picked up another one, handed it back.

Generations

At the end of an unseasonably warm day
New Year's Eve 2017
I stood in my kitchen holding
one wooden spoon.

My mom was watching TV
in the living room
eating apples, crackers, and cheese.
My grandson slept in a stroller
in a quiet back room.
I was related to both people,
ages ninety and one.
They were peaceful.
And that was it.
The most beautiful moment
of my life.

I'm Okay

For a longtime depressive
to adopt the anthem "I'm okay"
the last years of her life
was a gift.

Even when we found her passed out
with a full teacup on her chest,
even when she fainted
after drinking a giant margarita
or eating enchiladas
then climbing a hill
in a hundred degrees

she said no need
to call an ambulance,
Just help me up, please.
Seriously, I'm okay.
Seriously?
Mom!

What were we supposed
to do with such
changing weathers?

After the fuse of depression
blew out,
she described feeling
more alive.
She made decisions quickly,
I'm selling this house
I'm dumping this farm
but wasn't manic. It was all
miraculously okay
and a time like
no other in her life
or mine.

Friends kept showing up
to take her to lunch
in more than one city.
Her smile grew brighter,
she was hungry for fun.

Palestine Vine

Seeds wrapped tenderly in plastic,
one package said *White*, one *Red*.

Hand-lettered, mailed by friends
I never met.

They grew instantly.
Strangely confining themselves to one corner

of the metal container, as if a metaphor.
I swear I planted them all over.

Leafy vines popped forth,
glory and green lengthening overnight.

I didn't notice one had twined
around the rungs of the table.

Today, moving the pot,
the biggest vine ripped out, broke off.

No! How could I have missed the simple
wrapping of the tendril suggesting pleasure

in that exact light?
Its roots remain. A broken stem.

I wasn't evil, but I wasn't careful.
This is what happens in the world.

Now, soaking snipped vine in a glass of water, feeling
the hope and weight of so many years.

Always Be

In ninety-four years
my mother has said
many strange things,
but yesterday
the strangest.
When I leave here
maybe you can go with me.
What?
Like my neighbors did.
The daughter died
right after the mother,
everyone shocked.
She hadn't been ill.
Or my mom's Italian friends
who died the same day
not from an accident.
What?
We'll be together in heaven.
I don't think she believes in heaven.
At least, she didn't till yesterday.
She just wants me

to clean up after her,

what I did all my life,

sweeping crumbs,

scrubbing plates.

She'll always be

with me.

I prop her broom against

the wall.

Things We Don't Want to Remember

The day she ran over her favorite-ever cat.

The falls.

Her six mysterious hours
driving around
 "looking for cat food,"
returning with celery.
"I wasn't lost,
but I didn't know
where I was."

Stitches across a scalp.

The day she told EMS technicians
her name was Barack Obama.

They slapped hands and said,
"She seems okay to us!"

Things We Want to Remember

As a little girl, she was named
May Day Queen
for her elementary school,
given a shining ring of fragrant flowers
to wear on her head all day. Her crown.
Satin ribbons fluttering down.

Sign on Wall at San Francisco Zen Center:
Don't Waste This Life!

Next to the gong.
My mom would pause and place
her hands together in front of her.

Close her eyes.
Then lie down and sleep for three hours.

Small thoughts, small thoughts,
pigeons on the sidewalk.

Adore

A door
into a day.

Fire ate the body of my beloved father,
at which point he grew.
His life, her life, all of our lives,
the mountains and the open windows.

Miriam at the Blue Barn

In her last seven months
she wants only beauty,
blues and pinks,
woven shawls, steaming cup of tea,
candlelight, incense, Gregorian chants.

Lucky one, she has no illness,
just stops eating.
One day her body factory closes down.
She pushes away a hundred little plates.
Not even ice cream!
It takes seven months
for her cells to get the message.

Before that she says,
Let's drive to the Blue Barn,
fifty miles north of town, flower farm
operating on trust method.
Drop your cash and checks
through the slot of the old mailbox . . .

Herbs and blossoms in buckets and pots.
She sits on the porch in a rocking chair,
meditates on furrowed fields in sunlight.
One day she asks me to leave her there.
Imagine! With the hummingbirds.
In her blue-flowered dress.
Could they pick up this mysteriously
disappearing mama
with their tiniest beaks
and spirit her away?

Make it easier?
I fear the last days.

Forgiveness Circle

Before my mother died
I wanted to try something
I'd heard about. We sat out
on the porch together. I said,
I'll go first. Please forgive me
for losing my patience sometimes,
for pushing you when
you didn't want to
exercise or eat,
for not always being as sweet
as I should have been.

I paused to let her
take this in. Then I said,
It's your turn. She said,

I got nuthin'.

Veiled Miriam Naomi Leaves the Room

That was not you,
that bony disappearing person,
heave-ho shriek of pain,
sleeping for hours without any dreams,
inability to eat. You loved to eat.
That was not you.

You were the smile that flashed so brightly
climbing into bed again,
a mind still rich with exotic words,
gusto for teachings of swamis and saints,
affection for coupons,
patience with chaos.

You were the way we went,
the alley, the avenue, finding treasures,
always wanting to please.

In the end you were lifted by Buddha's quietude,
floating in a Gregorian chant,
drifting with sparrows who didn't even see you
sitting there, in your chair, in your bright red hat.

Conversations

Her doctor says, Let your discomfort
be your guide. Do what you feel like doing.
She says,
Sleeping!
Just let me sleep!

I ask for her favorite verbs.
She'll have to think about that.
Are there any she doesn't like?
Sure! Kill.
But I'm more a visual person.
No, you're not, Mom,
you do crossword puzzles!
She says that's different.

When she dies on Thanksgiving
right after sundown,
I remember how she loved
that old Thanksgiving song,
singing it over and over,

Over the river and through the woods,

to Grandmother's house we go.

She has gone on without us this time

and the forest is so dark.

Friends Are So Kind

Flowers, flowers, flowers.
They send many white flowers.
Living in a greenhouse feels comforting,
every table jammed. Frilly plants,
a box of homemade apricot preserves.
A wind chime and a weighted blanket.
Mama photographs we didn't have.
Notes, poems, cards.
One friend copies Darwish,
translated by Agha Shahid Ali,
both gentle men I loved, and knew,
who already died.
Are they welcoming her?
Palm trees have become weightless,
the hills have become weightless;
and streets in the dusk have become weightless . . .
Words have become weightless
and stories have become weightless
on the staircase of night . . .
So I float around for a few months.
The cat's tail sweeps me up.

Open Day

Are you standing by a window?

Pink stripes waking up sky

Birds balancing in bamboo

Demanding something of one another

Nothing of us, though

They need nothing from us

This is the first thing that should

make us happy

        ↄ૯

It's very cozy, living in

a notebook. You pull the pages

up over your head. Echoes of voices

find you. Some live inside,

others pull you out to the yard.

I miss everything I ever loved but it's

very near.

Before I End This Speech

What speech were you giving, Mom?

I find this strange phrase scrawled on the backs
of ten different envelopes.

Who was listening, Mom?
Did we ever listen well enough?
Does anyone?

Last week, completing one task
after your death
you had long ago requested,
my phone chimed. Your face came up
smiling, as if you had texted me,
something you never learned to do.
Then a whole photo stream
of your portraits cycled
with happy music. I felt you
in the room.

Was that a speech, too?
Were you saying, About time!

Yes, I would do anything for
one day more. You always hear people
say that. The speech goes on
inside the hearts of all who live.
It's in your little torn scraps,
pepper, olives, lemon, pimentos,
on the same page.

The Day the Big Tree Came Down

Old Grandpa Pecan had been dead so long,
we cheered.
We'd been fearing him, directly across
the street from our house.
What if he fell on our heads, our cars?
You sat in the porch swing with a serious face
and your fuzzy pink bathrobe
to watch him topple.

Like Daddy, you loved sitting outside
to smell the air.
A lady from down the street walked over
to tell us Amparo was dead.
Amparo, who kept a small chapel
of flickering candles and holy relics
in her backyard,
who decorated her tall blue and white house
for every holiday,
even ones we never heard of.
Amparo, our neighbor for forty years,
slipped away when we weren't looking.
She didn't want anyone to know.

You, mommy, *madre*, mum,

sat silent in the swing.

What were you thinking?

You didn't cover your ears

when the giant saw

seared off the looming section

we most feared. Arm by leg by neck.

Bit by bit, limb by leafless limb,

we said goodbye

to our friend

who had once shaded our block.

We Never Know

" . . . we never know who will be staying with us and who will be going

and how long it will be . . . "—Marion Winik

When the country fell apart,

I fell into poetry,

which cost nothing

but care.

And there,

in the empty pocket of the day,

found so many ways, again and again,

to think, to live, to be.

When the family dissolved,

one by one,

disappearing into death

or abandonment,

memories

planted themselves in odd places,

a sock drawer,

a lamp,

a hat.

Nothing required for
survival of memories
but a passing nod,
an endless love,
gratitude.

Leavings

Book as landscape
        topographical residence
   layers of years
Digging down through soil of pages
          fronds of words
    dreamy spaces   lost ages   the house without a roof

is floating
     it is not looking for its punctuation
when she died   the book remained resting
    on the small table beside her bed
              ꝏ
         I will meet you at the binding
       you became my binding
          we were bound together even without
   a reader
  feel my veins curling up a spine of days

        intentions crumpled
places we never went yet   stories broken

her memory lodged in the bottom of the cup she drank from

          while reading

Feel the shadow she casts   in our rooms

    as we keep translating   the lush and shifting light

Healing

Lean into it, the breeze suggests.

Dig deeper, says the dirt.

Sometimes the hurt you feel

means you're standing in the wrong place.

Move over.

This hurt wasn't meant for people.

It wasn't meant to land anywhere.

It's the cosmic ache of the atmosphere

drifting through, the give-and-take,

push-pull flow.

You know when it passes,

the lift of the air.

Hear the held note like

the quiet humming

an orchestra tunes to.

That's for you.

You Will Never Be Lonely Now

She is standing behind you in the doorway
watching you stride up the hill in rain boots.

Fantasy of shaping
another person.

The lost art
of perfect mothers.

I wanted to be everything
she wanted me to be.

Cherry tree full of gifts.
Row of silent shaggy pines

between our house
and the neighbors.

Steadfast through snow,
never bending.

Worry was her secret child.

It adopted her before we were born.

She tried to be its mother, too.

You could never tell it what to do.

New

If we spend more time with the dirt
everything else will hurt less.

Our own mistakes, rake the soil over.
Bone meal, vitamins. Where is the wisdom

we need? In that time after planting,
take a deep breath, step away.

A son moves out. A mama dies.
Polishing the shelves of their old closets,

you realize you didn't know what they were
storing. It's unexplored territory,

the beautiful grief
of all this new space.

Not Pass Away

I did not "lose" my mother.

The space
where the mother was
is very large

Vines still root themselves
in soft dirt

Pink roses pop open
in the cold

Even trees
whole trees
inhabit the space

speckled
light and shadow
a branch's embrace

say

look up

look out

everywhere

her home

now

The President Writes You Back

Six months after your death, a creamy envelope
pops into our box, addressed to you, return address,
THE WHITE HOUSE.
You would have cheered. For a whole month
you worked on your loving letter
of thanks to Joe Biden, saying his name
as if he were someone you knew,
without the "president" attached,
your old friend.
You bought sunglasses like his.
This was before he let Gaza be pummeled,
so many people who looked like the people
you loved, be erased. After mailing your letter,
you asked me to drive you
out of town, so you could thank the fields and sky
for being united. After the crazy years we'd all
lived through, such relief. And then you died,
and he wrote you back.
At least, someone in his office wrote you back.
What do I do with that?
That simple fact?

Moving On

I thought of you
before dawn
after so many had moved on
into invisible spaces
holding us
in their huge hands

After sky had cried
Birds! Birds! Birds!
to welcome back the light

Small movements of night
twig dropping
palm breathing into new frond

Settle down
It's like a new town
since you left
still bearing old clues

Sense

Traffic on the highway could be waves crashing against rocks.
Maybe we're seaside. Something soft over which
we have no control has entered the room.

Its name is Time
and it's your real parent.

Line up unfinished crossword puzzles on her bed.
She'll return to them later. Skinny pen clutched in her right hand
for *ogres, rue,* and *sense.* She'll think of something.

All the Places We Hadn't Gone Yet

The signs reach out and grab me.
Shambhala Buddhist Meditation Center,
some seafood shack on O'Connor Road.
You loved making a plan, looking
forward. It's very hard to drive
on Nacogdoches Road because of this.
Sylvia's Mexican Food with its
bright orange sign looked inviting,
but we never passed it
at the right time.
Your wishes reverberate.
The air still swarms with hope.
I was the driver, the chaperone, the lady-in-waiting.
There's the roadside stop where we unpacked
our Popo's lunch-to-go boxes
in a wild wind, and our napkins blew away.
You said,
We will really have to come back here
on a calmer day.

The Mail Goes On and On

Your *Mindful Magazine*
urges you to resubscribe.

Lion's Roar keeps roaring in
bidding us to take a journey,

focus simply,
remember all our gifts.

Right before you died,
you told me to renew it

for three years. Now it nudges
in its own quiet way.

She's here.
She's still here.

One

A delivery man pounded the door.
The boy said, That shook
my bones.

Only months ago,
before Covid happened,
on the brink, at the edge

I kept saying,
Something really big
and weird is about to happen.

My mama would later say,
This is the weirdest time
I saw in ninety years.

At his father's funeral in Libya,
everyone told Khaled,
Aye – zanah – wahad. Our grief is one.
Under the differences, beyond the many years

we did not speak together, *Wahad*.
When the sun sinks low, we will both
be watching it, perplexed.

I told the boy
I had a bad dream.
He said, Have a new one.

Not Very Much Inside

"Everywhere she dies. Everywhere I go she dies.
No sunrise, no city square . . .
but has her death in it."
                    —Norman MacCaig

I don't want to carry on like this.
Prefer, *Everywhere I go, she lives!*

The mother rolls grape leaves for an hour. Patience.
The mother stirs rice pudding for an hour. Patience.

She demonstrates for justice,
sits on the witness stand for her students.

Embroiders tiny petals on pillowcases late at night.
Not very much inside, but made for you with love.
It's the one note I'll really remember.

Sure, everyone had ups and downs.
Some lasted for decades.

We carry flash cards of one another's lives.

Texas Remedy

Step outside at twilight,
this sky won't wait.

Crushed wrapper blowing down the street,
release what snares you, then go chase that trash.

Answer rising egret with your own breath.
Yes, it's terrible, but the sky still looms

larger than any place you ever called
home. Remember what a door was for,

letting in people you love,
swinging wide still, when no one is there.

Now it's the wind's turn.
In Texas, always a wide chill coming

to change the sky before the ground.
Be patient, sure there's lots of bad around,

but more room for good, too, with all this empty.
Goats that don't freeze, thirsty rivers,

Ozona, Electra, and Alice, bearing
their own sorrows and staggering joys.

Blow a kiss to the far-off town
of your first real job,

Longview.
Pretend it branded you.

An Inch of a Word

Your great-grandson
reminds me of everyone.

He's funny like my dad.
Particular like you.

Don't you even say one inch
of a word about that!

And he's tender
as his own dad was,
and think, this is just
one branch of the family.

Necklace of glistening
cells, his mama's beauty,
his other grandma's deep calm,
we could go on and on
in this life

and so we do,

even after some of us are gone,

the mirror inside the mirror effect

which he calls scary when he's six.

But it's not scary really,

it's comforting. He speaks

and you wonder whose mouth

it's coming from,

I like to think about the clouds,

how they're always moving,

and they're so quiet.

I've been with you from the beginning.

If you don't say nice things

you shouldn't have a mouth.

He's the echo chamber,

the deep well into which

we pitched all our wishes

since we were born.

Everyone Looks Familiar Now

My neighbor asks me to get that strange man out of her yard.

Pounds on my door, he's here again, send him away.

I say, That's your husband, you've been together thirty-five years.

She won't be convinced. She wants to go home.

She wants her mother, sisters, everyone

who died a long time ago.

She wants my own mother

who's sitting on the couch.

She says she's going to the little house

and never coming back.

About this, she may be right.

We all are.

Tonight the young couple on bicycles

whizzing down the block

could be us,

forty years ago,

I swear I had that shirt.

And the man who trained his dog Henry

in the park for months during the pandemic

seemed so familiar,

I missed him every day when he left.

How do you miss someone

you don't even know?

Who are we all, in the big picture?

We grew up

in a blur of green hope so reckless,

it's a miracle we made it this far.

When Connor says

kids are *funner* than adults,

it seems my sweet dead father

is speaking through him again.

How can we live without being confused?

Just know we're not alone and never were.

It's okay to answer to many names.

We came down a long train track,

then sat there stuck while patient cars on both sides

waited at the signal. And every person

had something similar going on,

hungry, impatient, or scared,

we were all full of hope.

Why didn't those drivers U-turn toward

the one street with an overpass?

It's always been too easy to give advice.

Box of Ashes

Take me to the Buddhist hillside, she said,
to the place I was happiest
sitting and reading for hours
in a weathered wooden chair.

Rushing creek,
sifting breeze,
gently subtle garden,

leave me there.

Whisper Road

Small message trying to reach you.
From where, from where?
Minor breeze rounding a corner.
How could it be
the air we never see
can feel like our best friend?

Blossom

Who were we then?

We will always be
those people.

We can never be
those people again.

How many times did
the mother remember her days
before mothering?

Does the blossom recall the bud?

In our button box
lives one large black-and-white button
which sometimes escapes
to be found in a strange place,
cat litter box, silverware drawer.
Who sends the message?
Do spirits write letters like this?

So much hope
gathered around
another person—

who you might
become,
how you might
unfold.

In Morning

The Palestinian child

does not think about being Palestinian,

only of how his kitten

slept last night

and why is it not

in its basket.

Before he walks to school,

he will find it playing

with neighbor kittens

outside his house

and make sure it has breakfast.

The Ukrainian child

checks her doll

in its crib

which is really a box

for shoes

and tucks

the blanket

which is really a napkin

tighter.

The Libyan child
thought he lived in a desert,
so how could his house wash away,
the Moroccan child
never dreamed an old building
with such fat walls
could fall,
the child of Maui
never wears socks
but someone has given him
socks.
He misses
his messy room
which he would clean up right now
if he still had it.

Each morning
we put ourselves together.
Try to imagine
what we will do,
gathering tools and
thoughts.
We carry the mysteries

no one explains.
Scary things
feel farther away
in morning.
We try not to worry.

Wash face
brush teeth,
be as good as possible
because the stones
lined up
by the grandfathers
are still somewhere
and the wind from the west
is still your friend
and the little gray bird
pecking at a crumb
said something
we almost understood.

Acknowledgments

Conestoga Zen, edited by Rustin Larson; *Jung Journal: Culture & Psyche*; *Tikkun*; *Oneing: Unity and Diversity*; Queensland Poetry; *De Natura Libris*, by Álvaro Alejandro López; *University of Portland Magazine*; *Narrative*; *Soundings East*; *Reverberations:two, a Visual Conversation*, Sebastopol Center for the Arts; *Leaning Toward Light, Poems for Gardens & the Hands That Tend Them*, edited by Tess Taylor, Storey Publishing, 2023; *Texas, Being: A State of Poems*, Trinity University Press, edited by Jenny Browne, 2024.

I'd like to thank my wonderful editor, Virginia Duncan; great copyeditor, Tim Smith; visionary art director, Paul Zakris; and beautiful artist Lynne Avril for their contributions to this book.

Also, I'd like to thank our recent evening companions, possibly the two best television series ever made, both about families: *Dickinson* and *This Is Us*. They are works of art and highly recommended!

"What do ghosts eat for protein? Candles?"—Connor James Nye

Index of First Lines